Get up to Speed Quick in Node.js

in under 100 pages

by Joel Recinos

To Jordan, a future programming genius.

TABLE OF CONTENTS

Who this Book is For?

I envisioned this book helping in two kinds of programming scenarios. One would help beginning JavaScript programmers looking to land a job as a node.js developer. The other would be experienced programmers who need to quickly learn the basics of node.js for a new project.

This book requires that you are familiar with JavaScript syntax, and a basic understanding of a REST API. It also requires that, if you are not using Mac, that you are savvy enough to know how to apply the same concepts to your Windows box.

Also, any text appearing inside a gray box is meant to give more in-depth background of a key technology.

Buzz Words

Buzz words are important words or jargon phrases in the technology industry. Buzz words will appear throughout the text in bold font. So it would be wise to understand, and remember, explanations for these terms. They are also worth mentioning during an interview for a developer position. It is especially important to understand them in case an interviewer asks you to explain them.

CHAPTER 1 – WELCOME TO NODE.JS

Node.js is not a programming language. JavaScript is the programming language used to build node.js applications. Node.js is a **framework** built on JavaScript. A framework is a software foundation so you don't have to write all the application code from scratch. Node.js lets you write *server* applications using JavaScript, which was previously unheard-of because JavaScript was mostly a client-side language that ran scripts only inside a client's browser. Node.js is expandable because it lets you choose third-party 'helper' applications (called 'packages'), so you don't have to write code to do common things like handling web requests, or serve HTML to clients. Node.js has packages, like EJS, Mustache or React, to generate HTML web pages to serve to a client's browser.

If you've ever loaded a web page in your browser, you know that the code for that web page comes over the internet from an external web server. Node.js lets you develop server applications by running a web server right on your laptop. This lets you serve up web pages directly to a web browser on your laptop by using the "localhost" domain.

For example, you would write your node.js server app and configure it to be served over the port of your choice, such as port 8080. Then you would open your web browser, and access your node app by going to http://localhost:8080

PORTS

Whenever you open your browser and type in a web address, you are implicitly connecting to the web server on port 80. Port 80 is the default port for serving-up web pages. By 'default', it means if you don't type in a port number, it defaults to port 80. So when you serve node.js apps on your laptop, you could choose port 80, but its best to choose a different port, to avoid conflicts with any other processes running on your laptop that may have commandeered port 80. A common alternative is to use port 8080. So keep in mind, if you use a port other than 80, you must type it in your web browser, with a colon after the domain name.

For example, to access a theoretical web page on port 60 of google.com, you would open your browser and go to https://www.google.com:60

INSTALLING NODE.JS

Go to https://nodejs.org

A NOTE ABOUT INSTALLATION INSTRUCTIONS

As you go thru a career in software development, you will often read software installation instructions that are out of date, or downright obsolete, because the software company has since changed their website layout. Quite often you will come across these stale instructions via google. They might tell you to click on links that no longer exist. You have to expect this as a software developer, and learn to find things on your own. Look for links on a website named 'download' or 'install' and then read the instructions for yourself. Reading and understanding the written word (comprehension) is a vital skill you must develop to become a successful software engineer who 'gets up to speed fast' and 'works well with little supervision'. A ‘self-starter’ can hunt for the info they need without bothering the lead tech.

Hopefully the node.js web site will automatically detect your operating system (OS) from the browser's 'user agent' and redirect you to a page titled "Download for macOS".

There should be two choices to download: the LTS version and the current version.

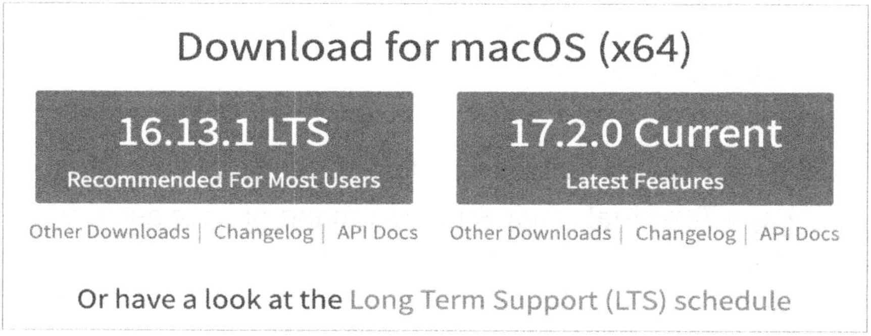

LTS

Most software will offer these two download options: LTS and Current/Latest. So it's good to under stand what LTS means.

LTS stands for **Long Term Support**. It identifies the latest *stable* version -- that is, tried and true, and mostly bug-free. The *current* version may include some new features that may still contain hidden bugs.

LTS means the software development team is committed to keeping this version of the software maintained and updated for a long period of time, usually 3 to 5 years.

For this reason, download the LTS version of node.js. It should download a file called "node-v16.13.0.pkg" to your hard drive (version numbers may differ). Go to the Finder and look for the downloaded file (probably in your 'downloads' folder) and open it (by double-clicking it). It will pop open a window to install. Follow the instructions, and when install is complete, you may move this file to the trash.

Check to see if node.js installed correctly on your laptop by opening a **Terminal** window (or command-prompt as they are called in Windows).

To open the Terminal on MacOS, click the "Launchpad" icon in the Dock bar. In the search box, type: terminal. Click on the Terminal icon when it appears. Right-click on the Terminal icon in the Dock bar, and select "Options -> Keep in Dock". You will use Terminal a lot, so it makes sense to keep it handy in the dock.

By the way, commands in this book that are meant to be typed in the terminal window are displayed after an “>” character (but don’t type the “>” character).

Enter the command below in the terminal window:

```
> node --version
```

It should display the version you just downloaded. This lets you know node.js was installed correctly.

NPM

Installing node.js also installs the **Node Package Manager** (**npm**). NPM is a powerful tool for installing third-party applications, called ***packages*** into your node.js project. Windows developers can think of packages as being similar to external DLL’s or external libraries. Packages give your node.js app additional features and functionality. For example, you will need to install the '**express**' package in your node application to be able to handle and serve web requests. To make sure npm was installed, check the version in your terminal:

```
> npm --version
```

It should display the current version of npm, but its also letting you know npm was installed correctly.

We will use other npm commands later to initialize a project and to install packages. But for right now, we just want to make sure npm is installed and working.

CHAPTER 2 - CREATE THE PROJECT

Now you are ready to start your first node project. A skill you will use again and again is, consuming a REST API from an external website and displaying its data on your website. In our case, our node.js project will pull hockey data from an external api and display it on a web page.

API

API stands for **application programming interface**. It's usually a set of classes or functions that a software team exposes to the public to allow other developers access to the software library's features and functionality. For example, the code you write would call these api functions or use their classes in your own code. Nowadays, these "software libraries" are mostly online and accessed via the internet. They are still called api, except you must use a format like REST to call their functions over the internet. More on REST later.

Once our node.js hockey app is complete, we will create a GitHub account and add this project to our GitHub portfolio (more on that later). Having your code projects on GitHub.com allows prospective employers to view your code to get an understanding of your programming knowledge and skill level.

Whenever you learn a new programming language, it's a good idea to learn its syntax by developing an application that calls an external REST API and parses the data. Most REST

API's in this day and age return JSON data. An old legacy REST API may still return XML data, or maybe SOAP formatted XML, but most companies have converted their RESI API's to return JSON data. So that is what we will focus on working with: JSON data.

JSON

On a basic level, JSON is a data format (not a programming language). Data is JSON is either a JSON 'object', surrounded by curly braces { }, or a JSON 'array', surrounded by square brackets [ ]. Either can contain the other. JSON objects contain 'keys' and 'values', which are separated by colons. Each key/value pair is then separated by commas. The 'key' (name) must be in quotes. The values can either be a string in quotation marks, or a number (without quotation marks), or a boolean true/false (without quotation marks). The JSON below contains all three types, as well as an array of two objects:

```
{
        "company" : "ACME Software",
        "employees" : 2394,
        "active" : true,
        "officers" : [
                {
                        "name" : "Pat Jones",
                        "title" : "President"
                },
                {
```

```
                "name" : "Chris Jones",
                "title" : "CEO"
            }
        ]
}
```

JSON data cannot be used as-is on a web page. It must be parsed. Parsing, in this instance, means converting the JSON data into something your website can use by extracting the pieces of data you want. For example, if you call the NHL's REST API looking for a list of all the team names in the league, the JSON results may also contain tons of other data that you don't need, such as a team's won/loss record, or attendance figures, or names of its executive officers. So you have to parse the data and extract only the team names to display on your website. So, lets create our project.

Create a new directory in your home directory to store our node.js project. Use the Unix/Linux "make directory" command in the Terminal window.

> **mkdir** node

Change into the directory using the Unix/Linux change directory (cd) command:

> **cd** node

Now we need to create a project directory. It is important to use a project name that is suitable to use for your GitHub portfolio. Since we want to highlight our understanding of consuming REST API's to display hockey data from an external web site on our web page, create a new directory by entering the command:

```
> mkdir hockey-api
```

Change into the directory using the cd command:

```
> cd hockey-api
```

Now you're ready to create your first node application. The quickest and easiest way to do that is to use NPM to create a bare-bones application. In your terminal window, enter the command:

```
> npm init -y
```

You *could* leave out the -y 'flag', but then npm would require you to type in answers to a bunch of setup questions. The 'y' flag means to answer 'yes', or to use the default answer for all questions.

Take a look at the files created in your project directory by using the Unix/Linux command 'list files' (ls) in your terminal:

```
> ls
```

You'll see, only a file named 'package.json' was created. Told you it was bare-bones. **Package.json** is a 'config' file. A '**config**' file is a file that stores the settings, or values, needed to run, and/or customize, a software application. For example, if you install the 'express' package, the package name would be listed in the 'dependencies' section of the config file. But more on the package.json later. A whole book could be written just on all the package.json settings. A lot of config files will end in '.config' extension, or have no extension at all. NPM uses the JSON format for its config file, so its config files ends in '.json'.

You will need a directory to store your source files, so create a source directory. A standard name for this is 'src'.

> mkdir src

Now we're going to create our first source file *inside* the src directory using the Unix/Linux '**touch**' command below. Touch is actually a program to edit text files, but if a file doesn't exist, 'touch' will create blank file. Notice we added 'src/' before the file name. This is called the 'path' and in the Unix/Linux/MacOs world, a slash separates directory names and file names. The slash lets the 'touch' command know to create a new file called 'test.js' inside the 'src' directory.

> touch src/test.js

In the Unix/Linux/MacOs world, it is common to type the full path name so you don't have to first 'cd' into the directory. You can use a path in the 'ls' command to see all the files in a sub-directory from the current directory (trailing slashes not necessary). For example, to view the files inside the 'src' directory, without changing into the directory, enter the command:

```
> ls src
```

Now, let's install our first package using npm. Remember, we will need the 'express' package to handle and serve web requests. Let's install express by entering the command:

```
> npm install express --save
```

Notice above, that after the ‘npm’, we type the *install* command followed by the name of the package we want to install. The '--save' means the package name will written to the package.json file. This means anyone we give our source code will be able to run the 'npm install' command to install all the same packages we have listed in our package.json file.

We also need to install the axios package. **Axios** allows us to make REST API calls to external web sites to get data.

```
> npm install axios --save
```

Now if you run the 'ls' command to see the files in the directory, you will notice a '**node_modules**' folder. This folder contains all the third-party packages you installed, all in one convenient place. If you looked inside the 'node_modules' folder, you would expect to see two folders for 'axios' and 'express'. But actually there are over fifty folders! This is because both 'express' and 'axios' automatically dowloaded other packages it needed to run. These are called '**dependencies**'. (That is a good buzz word to remember.)

It is easy to see why the 'node_modules' folder can grow in size to several gigabytes. So if we deploy, or give our app to someone else, we would *not* include the 'node_modules' folder because it can easily be re-created from the package.json file by running the 'npm install' command from the terminal.

In fact, why not try it? In the Finder, move the 'node_modules' folder to the trash, then go to the terminal and type:

```
> npm install
```

Viola! The 'node_modules' folder gets re-created.

CHAPTER 3 – WRITING CODE

IDE

At this point, it is time to write some code. You do this with an **Integrated Development Environment** (**IDE**). This is a fancy word for text editing software specifically made for writing code. There are many good IDE's to write code on the Mac, like IntelliJ, Sublime Text and Visual Studio Code. We will use **Visual Studio Code** because you will often see this as a required skill in job descriptions. Sometimes it is just referred to as **VS Code**.

To install Visual Studio Code, type it in google or go to https://code.visualstudio.com/

> Be careful *NOT* to download the **Visual Studio 2019** IDE (or any other year). Even though they have similar names, and are both made by Microsoft, Visual Studio 2019 is meant to develop Windows applications, primarily using Microsoft's C# programming language. **Visual Studio Code**, on the other hand, lets you write code for different operating systems using many different programming languages such as JavaScript, Python, DotNet Core, Angular, and many many more.

Clicking the download link for Mac saves a zip file to your hard drive. If you go to the Finder and double-click on the zip file, it extracts a 'Visual Studio Code.app' file. Using the Finder, drag this file into your 'Applications' folder and double-click it to launch. Once VS Code is opened,

Choose menu: File -> Open

and browse to your node.js folder. Double-click on the node folder to reveal the 'hockey-api' folder. Click ONCE on the 'hockey-api' folder to select it, then click the "Open" button. (Click yes to 'trust the author' because the author is you.)

We selected the 'hockey-api' folder to open because the folder and its contents will be conveniently displayed in the left-hand navigation panel.

HELLO WORLD

Double-click the 'package.json' file to open it in the editor. (Note that if we *single-click* a file, it will open in a tab window, but it will be replaced by the next file you click.)

Notice in the 'dependencies' section of the 'package.json' file, the package names 'express' and 'axios' are listed (because we used the '--save' flag when we installed them with npm).

Leave the ‘package.json’ file open and click on the 'src' folder to expand it, then double-click on the 'test.js' file.

It is true that I could have uploaded all the source code files to GitHub so you could copy and paste the code to save you some time. But I really think you learn faster by typing out the code yourself. Besides that, when you're on the job, no one is going to type your code for you, so you better get used to it now. Enter the code below, exactly as it appears, into the 'test.js' file:

```
require('http').createServer((req, resp) => {
    resp.end("I am a genius!");
}).listen(8080);
```

So what does this code do? It is actually three function calls all mushed together (and technically a fourth function is passed as a parameter, explained later). The first function call, require('http'), is used to tell node that we want to use the ‘http’ module (which is needed to create a web server). The 'require' function is called whenever you want to use a 'module' or package. If you’ve been paying attention, you’ll wonder why we didn't have to use npm to specifically install an 'http' package. Its because node comes with a few pre-installed modules, one of which is called 'http'.

DIFFERENCE BETWEEN MODULES AND PACKAGES

A **module**, or library, is a single .js file, such as http.js. A package consists of one or more modules, along with a package.json file.

The require() function, which is ended by the ‘dot’ character, returns an object that can be used to call other functions defined inside the ‘http’ module. This object represents our ‘web server’.

The second function call, after the dot, is to the createServer() function. Notice the createServer() function accepts only one parameter, another function spanning three lines. When you pass a function as a parameter to another function, it is called a '**callback function**'. Basically, it is a function that runs later. In this case, the callback function will run when a web request actually comes in. When it does, the callback function calls the end() function of the 'resp' object which sends data to the browser. The data being sent to the browser is just one line of text, in lieu of an entire html page.

The third function call, after the dot, is to the listen() function to tell the web server to 'listen' on port 8080, for any incoming requests from a browser for a web page. Remember, that an incoming request for a web page will trigger the callback function.

This 'dot' syntax for combining function calls is called 'chaining'. It is basically a shorthand way of writing the full code in its longer syntax, as shown in the following example:

```
const http = require('http');
const server = http.createServer((req, resp) => {
      resp.end("I am a genius!");
});
server.listen(8080);
```

Notice the longhand version instantiates two class objects named 'http' and 'server', but ultimately calls the same functions as the shorthand version. Personally, I think the longhand version is easier to read and understand, but once you get a little experience under your belt, you might find yourself writing the quicker shorthand version to save time, and lines of code. The ability to rewrite programs with fewer lines of code is held in high regard in some programming circles. In any event, you will most-likely see both syntax forms in your JavaScript career.

Now, I am sure you are waiting to see the fruits of your labor. So let's run this app to see it displayed in a web browser. To do that, we could run the 'node test.js' command in terminal. But the standard way is to configure a 'start script' in the package.json. Open package.json in the IDE. Find the "scripts" section, add a new line, and type:

```
"start": "node src/test.js",
```

Don't forget the comma at the end. The JSON format requires it. The 'start' name is significant because that is what we must type in the terminal.

The "scripts" section should now look like this:

```
"scripts": {
  "start": "node src/test.js",
  "test": "echo \"Error: no test specified\" && exit 1"
},
```

Go to the terminal and enter the command below:

```
> npm start
```

NPM will look in the package.json file for a property named "start" and run the command next to it. (We could have named "start" anything, like "go-for-it", and then we would have run the command "npm go-for-it". But using "start" is the standard naming convention.)

Now open up a browser and go to: http://localhost:8080

(Make sure you do NOT type 'https', because the https protocol requires a security certificate on your server, which you probably don't have on your laptop.)

If your browser displays 'I am a genius!', it's because you are. Congratulations. You wrote your first basic node app (keep in mind, we did not yet use the Express or Axios packages we installed). This app will hardly impress your boss or a prospective employer. So, let's develop a simple project that will.

Back in your terminal, type **Control-C** to stop the node server so we can develop our next app.

HOCKEY APP

Go back to VS Code. Right-click on the 'src' directory and choose 'New File'. Name it 'server.js' and press the enter key.

A more modern way to 'require' a package is to use the 'import' statement. The ‘import’ keyword is part of the JavaScript language spec known as ES6, while 'require' is not (more on the spec later). The full syntax for the ‘import’ statement is:

```
import object-name from 'module-name'
```

Oftentimes the object name and module name are the same. Other times, the object name can be a *function* name or *variable* name or *object/class* name. Sometimes, you will need to import multiple objects from a single module (.js file). Then you would use this syntax:

```
import { variable-name, function-name } from 'module-
name'
```

Node doesn't support the ES6 'import' statement natively (out-of-the-box). You need to configure node to recognize it by:

1) enable this setting in package.json by adding:

"type" : "module",

Don't forget the comma at the end.

2) Also change the *value* of the "scripts" -> "start" property to "node src/server.js".

So your package.json file should now look like this:

```
{
  "name": "hockey-api",
  "version": "1.0.0",
  "description": "",
  "main": "index.js",
  "type": "module",
  "scripts": {
    "start": "node src/server.js",
    "test": "echo \"Error: no test specified\"
&& exit 1"
  },
```

```
  "keywords": [],
  "author": "",
  "license": "ISC",
  "dependencies": {
    "axios": "^0.24.0",
    "express": "^4.17.1"
  }
}
```

Now you can import the Express module on the first line of code in server.js.

```
import express from 'express';
```

Hit the return key a couple times to skip down to line 3 where we will instantiate an Express object named 'app' and use it to call the other functions in the Express module.

```
const app = express();
```

On line 4, we initialize a constant variable to hold our desired port number.

```
const port = 8080;
```

On line 6, we tell Express we want it to process incoming payloads as json. The Express use() function is called to load any middleware functions. **Middleware** is the term for software that takes input, modifies it, or transforms it, or converts it, and sends its output to the input of the next function.

```
app.use(express.json());
```

On line 8, enter the following code to tell Express to listen for incoming requests on the port defined in the 'port' variable (8080). The second parameter is a callback function to send a message to the terminal that provides the user with a url to paste in the browser to access our node app.

```
app.listen(port, () => {
    console.log(`Hockey app listening at
                    http://localhost:${port}`);
});
```

ROUTES

On line 12, we begin writing our routes. But first, we must talk about routes, what they do, how to run them, and how they correspond to REST API.

Routes allow your web server to handle http requests from the browser (or other clients). Routes **map** the path in url's to specific functions in the code, per the given REST API 'http verb' (more on REST HTTP verbs later).

> The **path** in a url is everything after the domain name, up to any "?", which indicates querystring parameters. **Map**, in this context, means to correspond one thing to another.

For example, given this url:

https://www.nhl.com/info/nhl-awards-trophies

The url path would be:

/info/nhl-awards-trophies

For this example url, you would need to define an Express 'get' function to match the url path, as shown in the code below. Notice the Express get() function takes two parameters. The first is the url path. The second parameter is a callback function. When a request is received, the callback function below would generate the proper html to send to the browser, or in this case, send a simple text message to the browser.

```
const path = '/info/nhl-awards-trophies';
app.get(path, function (req, res) {
      res.send('this is content for awards page');
});
```

If there is no path in the url, for example, the home page https://www.nhl.com/, then the path would just be a single slash:

```
app.get('/', function (req, res) {
      res.send('this is content for home page');
});
```

This home page callback, when it runs, would send a simple text message back to the browser.

A BRIEF REST API OVERVIEW

If you search “REST API” on Amazon.com, the results show entire books can be written about the REST API specification. It is a huge topic, so I will cover just enough to give you a basic understanding of how to handle REST API calls made to your web server (requests), as well as make REST API calls to other external web servers (consume).

The REST API specification defines eight **HTTP Verbs**. The four most frequently used are GET, POST, PUT and DELETE. (These HTTP Verbs are also called ‘methods’, but I will refer to them as 'verbs' so as not to confuse them with JavaScript class methods.) For now, just understand the four main verbs and the explanations below on what they are used for. Later I will show you how to use them in code to make, or handle, a REST API call.

The **GET** verb is used to *fetch* a resource from the server (A server resource could mean any type of data -- html file, images, database record, etc.)
The **POST** verb is used to *create* a new resource.
The **PUT** verb is used to *update* an existing resource.
The **DELETE** verb is used to *delete* an existing resource.

The REST specification is designed so that you can call the same url path, but with different HTTP verbs, and they would map to a different function in your JavaScript code to perform specific work for each verb. For example, you might have five Express routes defined in a code module to handle the five calls below, for (2) GETS, a POST, PUT and DELETE:

A **GET** call to **http://example.com/customer**
would return a *list* of customers.
A **GET** call to **http://example.com/customer/100**
would return a *single* customer for id 100.
A **POST** call to **http://example.com/customer**
would *create* a new customer.
A **PUT** call to **http://example.com/customer/100**
would *update* info for customer id 100.
A **DELETE** call to **http://example.com/customer/100**
would delete customer at id 100.

BODY

When using the POST or PUT verb, the call must include the data needed to add or update the resource, such as a customer's name, address, etc. The data is included in what is called the '**body**' of the request. The body is usually in JSON format. Here is what a JSON body for a customer might look like:

```
{
    "name": "Bob Jones",
    "state" : "California"
}
```

ID PARAM

Notice three of the example urls above (for PUT, DELETE, and one GET) contain a number at the end. This is an id number used to target a specific customer's data record to delete or update. Each web site would assign its own record id numbers to customers to keep track of them.

It's important to remember, we use the **Express** package to handle REST API requests to *OUR* web server. And we use the **Axios** package to make REST API calls to *OTHER* (external) web servers. So, for the five example urls given previously, we would need to write code for four routes to handle the four different verbs used. The routes would look like this:

```
app.get('/customer/:id?', function (req, res) {
    if (req.params.id) {
        res.send(`here is customer
                                  ${req.params.id}`);
    } else {
        res.send('here's a list of customers');
    }
});

app.post('/customer', function (req, res) {
      console.log(req.body.name);
      res.send('created new customer');
});
```

```
app.put('/customer/:id', function (req, res) {
      console.log(req.body.name);
      res.send(`updated customer
                               ${req.params.id}`);
});

app.delete('/customer/:id', function (req, res) {
      res.send(`deleted customer
                               ${req.params.id}`);
});
```

Let's look closer at the preceding code. Recall that 'app' is our Express instance that we use to call the functions inside the Express package. Notice the function names in bold -- get(), post(), put() and delete() – match the REST API http verbs.

Also notice that the get(), put() and delete() functions all have '/:id' in the path. The colon lets Express know that the url will contain a value which needs to be mapped to a variable named 'id'. This value would be the id number appended to the end of some of the example urls. Express will only handle the request if the url matches a defined path. So a PUT request with a url of '/customer/100' would match the put() route path and the code would be run. A PUT request *without* an id in the url '/customer' would not match the put() handler (because it is defined to expect an id), so nothing would happen.

So how does your code retrieve the value that has been passed in via the '/:id' parameter in the url? It's accessed inside the callback function via the request object named ‘req’, as shown in the delete() function. The Express request object has a ‘**params**’ property that stores all parameters passed in via the url string. Using ‘**dot notation**’ your code would fetch the value of id by specifying ‘req.params.id’. (**Dot Notation** lets you access an object’s properties (or field names) by separating property names with a dot.)

Besides a url parameter, there is a second way to pass data into a REST API handler: in the request body. If you recall, both the POST and PUT verbs require a body. In modern API’s, this is a JSON object. But how do you access values in the JSON body? By accessing the ‘**body**’ property of the ‘request’ object (much like the params property of the request object). This can be seen in the previous code in both the post() and the put() functions where we log the ‘req.body.name’ to the console (terminal).

So why does the path of the get() function handler have a question mark after the ‘id’ (‘/:id?’) in the url path? A question mark tells Express that the parameter is OPTIONAL. It may or may not be present in the url. Why do we need to make it optional? So it can match and handle requests for both ‘/customer/ as well as ‘/customer/100’. If you look at the code, the callback function passed to the get() function checks to see if the ‘id’ parameter is null or not. If the ‘id’ *is not* null, it sends back data for a single customer whose account number matches ‘id’ (assuming, of course, that we took the time to write the code to retrieve a customer's data). If 'id' *is* null (empty), it would send back a list of all customers to the browser.

Let's go ahead and write the needed code for the four customer handler functions on line 12 of the 'server.js' file (we will delete these functions later). We will need the server running for the next chapter, so start it via the terminal with the command below (if it's already running, type Control-C to stop the server, so it can be restarted using the latest code):

```
> npm start
```

PRO TIP

By the way, you don't have to keep typing 'npm start' in the terminal every time you want to restart your server. Just push the UP ARROW key on your keyboard and it will scroll thru all the recent commands you entered. Press the arrow key until the 'npm start' command re-appears, then press the ENTER key.

CHAPTER 4 – REST API

TESTING OUR REST API HANDLERS

A browser can only issue GET requests. After all its main job is to *get* a web page and display it. So how then do we test our code and call our server's get(), post(), put() and delete() REST API function handlers? Well, to call a REST API with POST and PUT verbs, every software developer needs a software tool such as cURL or **Postman** in their arsenal. These tools can call a REST API and display the JSON results. This lets you review the JSON property values to identify the data you want.

cURL

Some Unix/Linux superstars like to use a command-line tool called 'cURL' to make their REST API calls from the terminal window. But it is time-consuming and cumbersome to type out the long request on one line, much less having to remember all the correct flags for the command. Postman has an intuitive UI that makes it quicker and easier to do the same thing. So for that reason, we will focus on using Postman.

POSTMAN

There are actually two versions of Postman. A 'web version' that runs in your browser (you must create an account to use this version). And a 'desktop version' that you can download and install on your machine. I prefer the desktop version because I can quickly switch to it by clicking its icon in the Dock bar. By contrast, with the browser version, I would have to find the right browser window and then find the tab with Postman loaded. To download Postman, go to postman.com. Look for, and click, the link to 'download the desktop version' for your particular OS. I am sure you know how to install by now.

Once you have Postman up and running, you'll notice there is a navigation panel on the left-hand side and a data panel on the right. Click the big 'plus sign' icon near the top of the data panel to open a new window.

In the data panel, to the left of the url text box that says 'Enter request url', is a drop-down menu that let's you choose the HTTP VERB. Leave it at GET. Before we test call our customer handlers, let's use Postman to take a look at the external hockey REST API we will be calling from our node.js module. Paste this url in the text box and click the blue "Send" button.

https://statsapi.web.nhl.com/api/v1/teams

The JSON results are displayed in the bottom of the data panel. Your Postman UI should look similar to the following screenshot:

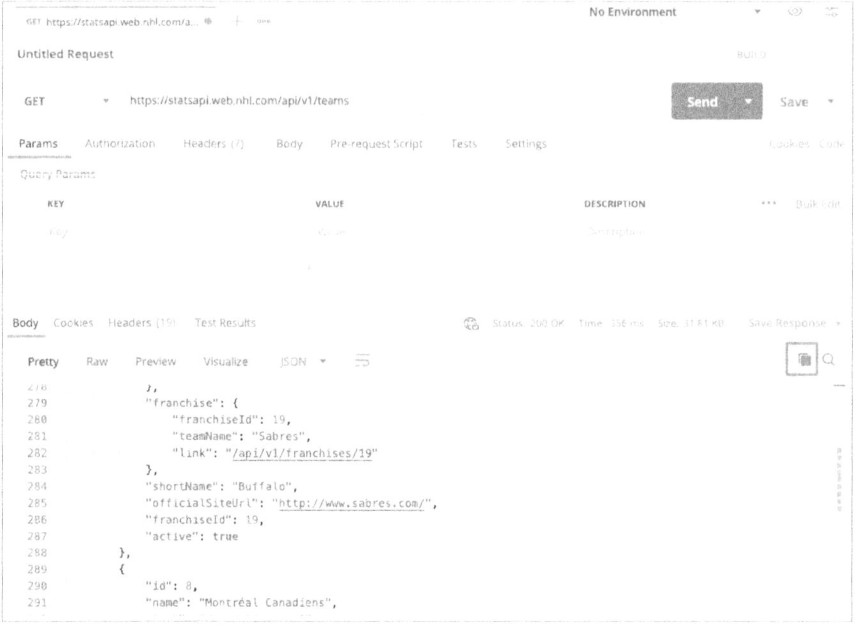

Click the 'copy' icon (on the right, marked with a square). This copies the JSON results to your clipboard. Now let's go to a handy online JSON formatter to inspect the results.

JSON VIEWER

Open a browser window and go to:

http://jsonviewer.stack.hu

Bookmark this site because you'll need to format JSON quite a bit during your career. Notice the website defaults to the 'text' tab in the display. Paste the JSON from Postman into the large text area. Then click the "Viewer" tab. This view collapses the JSON hierarchy in an easy-to-see format. Notice the square brackets next to 'teams'. Square brackets indicate a JSON array structure. A JSON array can contain one-or-more JSON objects. A JSON object is indicated by curly braces. Click the 'plus sign' next to 'teams' array to expand it.

It will display 32 JSON objects (indicated by curly braces) numbered 0-31. Each one represents an NHL team. To view team data you can either click on the name, or curly braces, of a JSON object. The key/value pairs inside the object will be displayed in the panel on the right, in alphabetical order. Or, you can also just click the 'plus sign' icon to expose the JSON object properties. If you look at the key/value pairs in the panel on the right, you'll see the data we want, the hockey team name, is located in the "name" property. Since 'teams' is an array, our code will have to loop through it and use dot notation to access the desired 'name' property. For example, if we expand the 'venue' object. The name of the arena where the team plays is located in the venue's 'name' property. To access this value in the code, we would iterate the teams array and use dot notation:

```
for (team of teams) {
    const venue = team.venue.name;
}
```

While we still got Postman open, let's call our local server's customer REST API to test how our code works. In Postman, click the plus sign to open a new window. Copy the url below to the url text box (leave the HTTP VERB menu set to 'Get') and click the blue "Send" button.

http://localhost:8080/customer

You should see the message ‘here is a list of customers’ as shown below:

Now append a customer id number to the url, as shown below, and click “Send”.

http://localhost:8080/customer/100

You should now see the message ‘here is customer 100’ in the results panel.

Now let’s test our PUT call.

1) Make sure the url still has the id number:
http://localhost:8080/customer/100
2) Click the GET verb and select PUT from the drop-down menu.
3) Click the ‘body’ tab underneath the url text box, then click the ‘raw’ radio button.
4) Enter the following JSON in the text box directly underneath the ‘raw’ button:

```
{
        "name" : "Bob Jones"
}
```

5) Click the "Send" button.

You see the response "updated customer 100" in the results panel, as shown in the screenshot below:

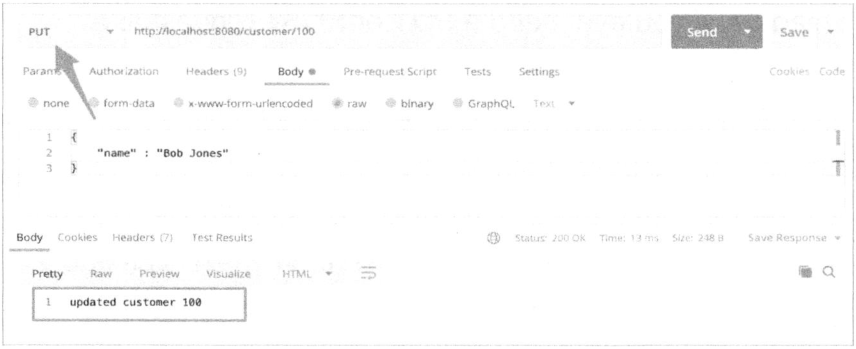

To test the post() function all you have to do is:

1) remove the id from the url:

    http://localhost:8080/customer

2) change the HTTP VERB to POST

    (remember, POST creates a *new* resource, so there is no need specify an id number.)

3) click the "Send" button.

You should now see the message 'created new customer' in the results panel.

And finally, to test the delete() function:

1) add the id back to the url:

    http://localhost:8080/customer/100

2) change the HTTP VERB to DELETE

3) delete the JSON from the body raw text box

(a 'body' is not needed for DELETE)

4) click the "Send" button.

You should now see the message 'deleted customer 100' in the results panel.

The last thing I want to mention about using Postman are the Headers. If you ever send a PUT or POST request to a known good REST API and it returns an error, you may need to set the headers to tell the external server what type of data you are sending it. We did not set headers for our simple examples, but you should make a habit of setting headers. It is easy to set headers in Postman. Click the 'Headers' tab (which is next to the 'body' tab). You'll see a grid with columns under 'Key' and 'Value'. Key is where we will type the header name, and Value is where we'll type the header's value.

We usually have to define two headers: 'Content-Type' and 'Accept'. '**Content-Type**' tells the server what kind of data we are sending to it, such as JSON or XML. To send JSON, the header should be:

Content-Type = 'application/json'

If you expect to receive data from the REST API, such as with a GET request, you should set the '**Accept**' header to tell the server what kind of data format you expect for the results. You don't want XML results if your code expects to parse JSON (luckily, most modern REST API's return JSON by default). To receive JSON, the header should be:

Accept = 'application/json'

The 'Headers' tab in your properly configured PUT request should now look like the screenshot below:

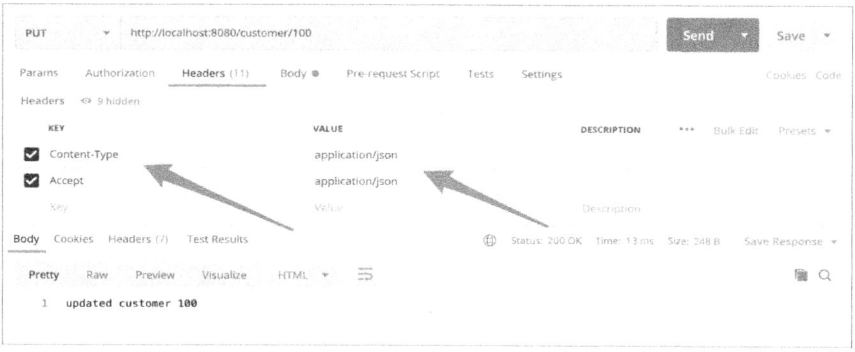

By the way, you should expect that third-party companies will eventually change the REST API without telling you. They might add authentication, causing you to add login credentials to the header of your API calls. Postman can certainly accommodate authentication headers.

Or, more commonly, they might add or remove properties you were counting-on and break your app. Sometimes they remove the API entirely, and you will have to search the internet for a new REAT API source. Sometimes they change the data type of a property. For example, the 'name' property used to be a simple string, but now its a string array. A change of data types will definitely break your code.

So if your code handlers suddenly start throwing an error, you now know how to use Postman to detect any changes in the JSON.

CHAPTER 5 - WRITING YOUR OWN MODULE

Now that we have covered the REST API basics, let's get back to our hockey-api program. Go ahead and delete all the customer functions that we added to server.js, starting with line 12. We do not need them any longer. (Or you can just comment out the code by typing a slash and asterisk '/*' at the beginning of line 12, and an asterisk and slash '*/' at the very end of the code on line 37.)

As demonstrated previously, you can define many routes in your module, including multiple get() handler functions. But for now, our hockey app only needs to handle the home page, with a url path of "/". The url from the browser would look like this:

http://localhost:8080

On line 12 enter this code:

```
app.get('/', function (req, res) {
      res.send('<h1>this is the home page</h1>');
});
```

Stop the server (Ctrl-c) and then re-start it with the command...

> npm start

Manually stopping and restarting your local server every time you edit the code can be a pain. Especially when you forget to do it and you can't understand why the code you just updated is not working in the browser. There are node packages available that will monitor your source files, detect code changes, and automatically restart the node app for you. But configuring them are beyond the scope of this small app. Just know that they are out there if you need them. You can find out more by searching for 'nodemon'. 'Webpack' can also do this for you but it is mainly a project bundler (for production deployment). So Webpack would have too much overhead just to monitor source files.

Open a browser window and go to:

http://localhost:8080

If you see 'this is the home page' in your browser, congratulations. You are ready to go to the next step.

It is best to keep your code segregated in separate files so that each file does only one major function. For example, the 'server.js' file spins up the server and handles server requests. Now we want to create a new file for our own module to handle the returned data from the external NHL REST API. It also needs to re-format the JSON data for display in a web page.

In VS Code, right-click on the 'src' folder and choose 'Add File'. Name it 'nhl.js'.

The first thing we want to do is import the Axios package so we can call external APIs. On line 1, type:

```
import axios from 'axios';
```

Then we define a *function* to *export* from our module so other files can call it. For example, we can *import* it, and use it, in 'server.js'. To export a function, add the 'export' keyword to the function definition, as shown in the code below. Enter this code on line 3 of 'nhl.js':

```
export async function getTeams() {

}
```

The 'async' keyword I will explain in a little bit more detail at the end of this chapter because it is part of a much larger coding paradigm of **asynchronous** programming. So, for right now, just know that if the code *inside* your function plans to call an asynchronous function (like when we call the axios.get function), you must precede the function call with the '**await**' keyword. For example:

await someImportantFunction();

Accordingly, if you use the 'await' keyword inside a function, then you must also decorate the function definition with the '**async**' keyword, as we did in the code on line 3. Those two keywords go together: async and await. But more on that later.

On line 4, enter the code below, inside the getTeams() function. It defines an empty string array that will eventually store all the team names we extract from the JSON results of the REST API.

```
let teamNames = [];
```

Next, we will use the Axios package to call the NHL api. On line 5, enter the code below.

```
const u = 'https://statsapi.web.nhl.com/api/v1/teams';
const results = await axios.get(u);
if (!results) {
    return teamNames;
}
```

Now, I could have just embedded the url inside the get() function, but then it would have been too long to fit on one line of this book. So I created a variable called 'u' to store the url on line 5. On line 6, we assigned the JSON results from the Axios call to a variable named 'results'. Notice we specified the 'await' keyword in front of the Axios get() function because it is an asynchronous function. If we forgot add it, the code would still run without errors, however, the code would not wait for the Axios call to finish, and the 'results' variable would never be assigned a value. The 'results' variable would always be null. I explain why at the end of this chapter. On line 7, we check to see if the 'results' variable is null (empty). If it is null, we cannot go any further and we should just exit the function and return the still empty array of team names.

If 'results' is not null, then we must write more code to process the data, which we will do shortly.

When you use Axios to call a REST API, the JSON data is returned in a property of the 'results' variable named 'data'. Since we assigned the Axios results to a variable named 'results', we would access the JSON data through dot notation: results.data.

And we know from using Postman, that the team data is stored in a JSON array named 'teams'. All we have to do is loop through the 'teams' array, and using dot notation, **push** (add) the team names into our string array. Enter the code below on lines 11-13:

```
for (const team of results.data.teams) {
    teamNames.push(team.name);
}
```

The last thing this module needs to do is return the results to the caller. So, on line 15, return the populated string array.

```
return teamNames;
```

Great job!

So your final code listing for 'nhl.js' should look like this:

```
import axios from 'axios';

export async function getTeams() {
	let teamNames = [];
	const u = 'https://statsapi.web.nhl.com/api/v1/teams';
	const results = await axios.get(u);
	if (!results) {
		return teamNames;
	}

	for (const team of results.data.teams) {
		teamNames.push(team.name);
	}

	return teamNames;
}
```

By the way, I do not normally like using one-letter variable names like I did with 'u' to store the url. But in this case I had no choice if I wanted to fit the code all on one line. The reason to avoid one-letter variables is because searching the code later for how and where this variable is used, can result in many irrelevant matches of the letter, in the middle of words. Yes, you can certainly modify the search to match case, but if you accidentally leave this on for the next search, it might unknowingly return less matches than expected.

ASYNCHRONOUS JAVASCRIPT

Why do we need Asynchronous JavaScript?

Sometimes, reading a file, or fetching records from a database, or running a large function can be '**expensive**'. That is, it takes too long to complete. These procedures can '**block**' the application from handling other requests. A web application might become unresponsive and the browser may appear to 'freeze'. When a web application is blocked, other HTTP requests cannot be handled and will 'timeout'.

Other programming languages and platforms solve this problem by creating a new 'thread' for these long-running procedures to run on, so the 'main thread' is not tied up. This is called '**multi-threaded**'. But node.js and JavaScript are single-threaded and cannot create new threads. So how does node.js avoid 'blocking'? The answer is asynchronous JavaScript.

Asynchronous JavaScript is a complex concept that is not easy for beginners to grasp. As a result, it is difficult to summarize in one or two sentences. So, I will start with an example to demonstrate how our node.js application can benefit from asynchronous JavaScript.

Suppose the home page our hockey website made *three* calls to an external REST API. One call would get a list of NHL teams that we would display as hyperlinks in the left-hand navigation panel. A second call would get a list of All-Star players that we would display in the content area. Underneath that, a third call would get a list of NHL hall-of-famers.

Our main code might call three different functions, as shown below, and then pass all three result variables to another function that would render the home page:

```
const teams = getTeamNames();
const allstars = getAllStars();
const hof = getHallOfFamers();
renderHomePage(teams, allstars, hof);
```

Suppose each call to a REST API takes about 1 to 5 seconds (ideally a REST API call should return results in milliseconds. But for simplicity, we'll use seconds). Normally, JavaScript runs in a **synchronous** manner. That is, the first function runs, and only when it completes is the second function called. When the second function completes, the third function is called. So in our hypothetical situation of a function taking 1-3 seconds to complete, if a user visits our home page, they might have to wait anywhere from 3 to 15 seconds for our home page to load before they see any content. Most users will get tired of waiting and browse to a different web site.

But what if we could run all three functions, at the same time, without any waiting. Then, whatever function finishes first, its content would magically display on the web page. Luckily, with asynchronous functions, JavaScript can do this. It can call the first method, but NOT wait for it to complete before it goes ahead and calls the second function. Then it could call the third function without waiting for the second function to complete.

This time, when a user visits our web page, whichever asynchronous function finishes first, that content will display on the home page. For example, the hall of famers list may appear first, followed by the team names in the left navigation, followed by the list of all-stars. No waiting for everything to load at once. Our users could start to see content in anywhere from 1 to 5 seconds (again REST API calls should ideally return results in milliseconds, not seconds. But you get the point).

How does JavaScript accomplish this asynchronous magic? Three different ways over the years: first was 'Callback Functions' (which we talked about previously). Then 'Promises' arrived in 2015, and finally 'Async'/'Await' in 2017. We'll take a closer look at each of these strategies a little later on. But first, a little JavaScript history is necessary to put these three strategies into perspective.

Evolution of the JavaScript Specification

JavaScript was introduced for the Netscape Navigator browser in 1995. JavaScript was quickly adopted by Microsoft for their new browser, Internet Explorer. Why is this important? Because Microsoft maintained their own version of JavaScript and added several **proprietary** features (meaning only available only in Internet Explorer). Eventually, this disparity in JavaScript engines grew until it was difficult for web site developers to write code that would run error-free on both browsers. Broken web sites caused by JavaScript errors was quite common in the late 1990's.

To solve this growing problem, it was decided that JavaScript should become a standard specification. All parties compromised on naming this new spec "ECMAScript". Starting in 2015, with the 6th version of the spec, the standards committee started releasing a new version every year. So this 2015 version was christened 'ECMAScript 2015', sometimes referred to as 'ES2015', or just plain 'ES6' (for the 6th version). This confusing versioning system is handy to know and understand.

Now let's take a little deeper look into the three versions of JavaScript asynchronous programming: callbacks, promises, and async/await.

Callbacks

You have already been using callbacks in your node.js code. Where? In your Express REST API handlers.

```
app.get('/', function (req, res) {
    res.send('this is the home page');
});
```

Callbacks are self-contained functions that are passed as a parameter to another function. In the code above, the callback is passed as the second parameter (remember, the first parameter is the url path). Basically, you are telling the Express get() function "I don't know when you are going to finish, but when you do, I want you to run this callback function." In the example callback above, it just writes a simple string of text to browser.

The code above is re-written below to help you better recognize that the get() function is accepting two parameters. For clarity, we assigned the callback function to its own variable:

```
//define the callback function and assign it to variable
const runThisCallbackLater = function(req, res){
      res.send('this is the home page');
};
//pass the callback function as a parameter
app.get('/', runThisCallbackLater);
```

Callbacks worked pretty good most of the time. But problems arise if you needed to nest multiple callbacks. For example, adding a second callback *inside* the first callback means the results from the nested callback are sent as input to the main callback. And so on if you add a third nested callback. Multiple nested callbacks can produce unintended hard-to-trace bugs if errors are not handled by the right callback. This was nick-named 'callback hell'.

Promises

Promises, introduced in ES6, was intended to be a better solution for asynchronous programming. A promise, in this context, is a promise by the asynchronous function to let the calling code know when it has finished. In our nhl.com REST API example, the Axios get() call promises to let the caller know when it has completed, so we can parse the JSON and extract the team names.

Promises typically look like the code below, with a then() function, and a catch() function to handle any errors:

```
const results = myAsyncFunction(myParams)
  .then((result) => {
    console.log(result);
    return result;
  })
  .catch((err) => {
    console.error(err);
  });
```

The dots before the then() and catch() functions mean that they are 'chained' to run after the myAsyncFunction() function in order. Think of chained calls like this:

```
myAsyncFunction().then().catch();
```

So, in the main code above, the myAsyncFunction() is passed data via the 'myParams' parameter, as normal. But when the myAsyncFunction() function completes successfully, the promises is said to be "resolved", and the 'then()' function is invoked. Any data returned from the myAsyncFunction() function, is passed into the then() function via the 'result' parameter (the param can actually be named anything).

If any error occurs in myAsyncFunction(), the promise is said to be “rejected”, and the catch() function is invoked. Any error messages are passed into the catch() function via the 'err' parameter (the param can actually be named anything, but the norm is usually ‘e’, ‘err’, or ‘error’).

The beauty of the promise is you can actually chain (add) multiple then() functions:

```
const results = myAsyncFunction(myParams)
  .then((result) => {
    console.log(result);
    return result;
  })
  .then((result2) => {
    console.log(result)2;
    return result2;
  })
  .catch((err) => {
    console.error(err);
  });
```

In this scenario, the results from the first then() function are then passed (promised) to the second then() function via the 'result2' parameter. Chaining then() functions ensure the second then() function is not called until the first then() function is complete. Promises make sure this expected order is enforced.

A natural question might be "How does the myAsyncFunction() function return a promise"? In most cases, when calling a third party asynchronous function, like the Axios get(), the third party developer has done this for you. But what if YOU were writing the asynchronous function? How would you get it to return a promise? Just return an instance of the Promise class, as shown below (it may look like a function that's being returned, but the 'new' keyword is not used with a function):

```
function myAsyncFunction(url){
  return new Promise((resolve, reject) => {
    SomeDatabase.connect(url, (err, db) => {
      if (err) {
        reject(err);
      }
      resolve(db);
    });
  });
}
```

Notice how the function calls either reject() or resolve(). Recall that a promise is "resolved" if the function is successful and "rejected" if there is an error. When writing an asynchronous function that returns a promise, *your* code must decide if the promise is returned to the caller as either resolved or rejected.

If you look closely, the Promise constructor (the code following 'new Promise') is actually passed only one parameter -- a callback function! So you can see why Promises are often thought of as a 'wrapper' for callback functions. In other words, the callback function in the Promise constructor basically adds Promise support to callback functions.

To further explain, here is the line of code (without the callback parameter) that instantiates the Promise class:

```
return new Promise();
```

Here is the rest of the code that serves as the callback function passed into Promise() constructor:

```
(resolve, reject) => {
  SomeDatabase.connect((err, db) => {
    if (err) {
      reject(err);
    }
    resolve(db);
  });
}
```

Let's look closer at the preceding callback function. When it is invoked (i.e. the code is run) it calls the function SomeDatabase.connect() which presumably makes connection to a database. The connect function is also passed a callback function that will be invoked when the connect() function completes.

The connect() function returns returns two values 'err' and 'db' that it passes as input parameters to its own callback function. If the connect() is successful, the 'db' object will have a connection to the database, and the 'err' will be empty (null). If an error occurs, the 'db' object will be null, and the 'err' object will have error data such as stacktrace and error messages.

The callback function evaluates these two parameters. If 'err' is not null, then there is an error, and it rejects the promise by calling the reject() function and passes it the 'err' object, so that it can be forwarded to the caller.

If the 'err' object is null (no error), then connect() is successful, the promise is ‘resolved’, and the 'db' connection object is returned to the caller.

Async / Await

Async and Await, introduced in ES8, is the latest solution for asynchronous programming. Just like a Promise wraps a callback function, Async / Await wraps a Promise. Some say it is merely '**syntactic sugar**'. Meaning the syntax may be easier to understand and look 'cleaner', but it offers the same functionality, under-the-hood, as the 'messier' and less-straightforward Promise code.

<u>Await</u>

The async/await keywords let you write asynchronous code that looks more synchronous, thus being easier to read, follow, and understand. It is easier to use than callbacks or promises. You merely add the await keyword in front of the asynchronous function. The await keyword lets JavaScript know that a promise will be returned.

```
const results = await axios.get(url);
functionThatProcessesData(results);
```

The thing to understand, is that if you forget the await keyword, JavaScript will call the Axios method, then immediately call the next function. Of course, the results variable will always be null, because JavaScript did not wait for the Axios.get() method to reach across the internet and return some data.

Async

Whenever you use the await keyword, it must be inside a function decorated with the 'async' keyword. The async keyword lets the caller know the function will run asynchronously.

```
async function callrestApi() {
      const results = await axios.get(url);
      functionThatProcessesData(results);
}
```

Catch

Remember that with promises, the .catch() function was chained in case anything went wrong. Well, in async / await, you will want to wrap your await code inside a try / catch block. That way, if any errors occur, it will be handled by the catch portion of try / catch block.

```
async function callrestApi() {
  try {
    const results = await axios.get(url);
    functionThatProcessesData(results);
  }
  catch(err) {
    console.error(err);
  }
}
```

CHAPTER 6 - IMPORTING OUR MODULE

To use the functions we just exported from our 'nhl.js' module (in the 'server.js' file), we need to import them by name. Open the 'server.js' file, and underneath the line to import Express, add the code below to import the getTeams() function from the 'nhl.js' module.

```
import { getTeams } from './nhl.js';
```

Then all we have to do is alter the Express get() function in 'server.js'. As shown below, add the 'async' keyword to the function declaration so that we can then use the await keyword before the call to the async getTeams() function. The string array eventually returned from the getTeams() function is assigned to a variable named teamNames. For right now, we are just going to log the team names to the console (terminal).

```
app.get('/', async function (req, res) {
      const teamNames = await getTeams();
      console.log(teamNames);
      res.send('<h1>this is the home page</h1>');
});
```

Let's run this puppy. Stop and restart the node app in the terminal. Open up a browser window and go to localhost:8080. Switch back to the terminal window and you should see results similar to the following screenshot:

```
hockey-api — node ◂ npm start NVM_RC_VERSION= TERM_PROGRAM=Apple_Ter...

> hockey-api@1.0.0 start
> node src/server.js

Hockey app listening at http://localhost:8080
[
  'New Jersey Devils',      'New York Islanders',
  'New York Rangers',       'Philadelphia Flyers',
  'Pittsburgh Penguins',    'Boston Bruins',
  'Buffalo Sabres',         'Montréal Canadiens',
  'Ottawa Senators',        'Toronto Maple Leafs',
  'Carolina Hurricanes',    'Florida Panthers',
  'Tampa Bay Lightning',    'Washington Capitals',
  'Chicago Blackhawks',     'Detroit Red Wings',
  'Nashville Predators',    'St. Louis Blues',
  'Calgary Flames',         'Colorado Avalanche',
  'Edmonton Oilers',        'Vancouver Canucks',
  'Anaheim Ducks',          'Dallas Stars',
  'Los Angeles Kings',      'San Jose Sharks',
  'Columbus Blue Jackets',  'Minnesota Wild',
  'Winnipeg Jets',          'Arizona Coyotes',
  'Vegas Golden Knights',   'Seattle Kraken'
]
```

If you see the team names in the terminal, congratulations Grasshopper. You are ready for the next step.

CHAPTER 7 - BUILDING THE HTML PAGE

Currently, our get() handler just sends a simple response to the browser using the send() function.

```
res.send('<h1>this is the home page</h1>');
```

This data string is a valid html 'h1' tag, and the browser knows how to render an 'h1' tag for display. However, it would be extremely laborious to write out an entire html document in a single line for the send() function. What we want to be able to do, is send our teams data to an html template file and have it return a fully finished html document that we can send to the browser.

Luckily there are many node.js packages that can do just that. Some of the more popular html engines are Mustache, Handlebars, Jade, Pug and even React. But for our simple app, we are going to use one of the oldest and easiest html engines called **Embedded JavaScript** (**EJS**).

First we need to install the EJS package:
> npm install ejs --save

Standard convention dictates that we keep our EJS template files in a folder called 'views'. Open VS Code, and look for the file Explorer on the left-hand side. If its not showing, click the Explorer icon that's at the top of the thin brown vertical navigation bar, as shown on the next page.

Right-click on any blank space in the Explorer panel and choose ‘New Folder’. Name the folder ‘views’ and press the enter key. Make sure the ‘views’ folder is now on the same level as the ‘src’ folder or the EJS engine will have a hard time finding its template files.

Right-click on the ‘views’ folder and choose ‘New File’. Name it ‘home.ejs’ and press the enter key. EJS template files must end with the .ejs extension.

An EJS file contains pure HTML with scripting tags embedded in them to generate the dynamic content.

Start by adding some basic HTML to the ‘home.ejs’ file:

```
<!DOCTYPE html>
<html lang="en">
  <head>
    <meta charset="UTF-8">
    <title>NHL Teams</title>
    <style>
      body { margin:0px; font-family: "helvetica,arial"; }
      #top-nav { background-color:#000080; width:100%; height:100px; }
      #wrapper { display:table; width:100%; }
      #left-nav { background-color:#000080; width:20%; }
      #main {background-color:#fff; width:75%; height:500px; padding:20px;}
      .row { display:table-row; }
      .row > div { display:table-cell; }
    </style>
  </head>
  <body>
```

```
    <div id="top-nav"></div>
    <div id="wrapper">
      <div class="row">
        <div id="left-nav"> </div>
        <div id="main">
          <h1>NHL Teams</h1>
        </div>
      </div>
    </div>
  </body>
</html>
```

CSS Selectors

Just a few words about CSS in the HTML template. In the “style” element, I use the ‘#’ selector to match the “id” attribute on those html elements that I know will only appear once in an html doc. Other devs like to use the “.” class selector (which match an html element’s “class” attribute) *for all styles*, even if the element already has an “id” attribute. Really, it’s just a matter of preference, though if you do use a style with ‘#’ “id” selector, an element with that id should only appear once in the html document. No two elements in a doc should have the same “id”. So, if you think you will be applying a style to more than one html element, use the “.” class selector and give the elements a “class” attribute.

In the “body” tag in the code above, notice there is a “div” with an id=”top-nav”. It will place a blue bar across the top of the page, simulating a top navigation bar. Then there is a “wrapper” div that contains the main content. Its CSS styles will set its “display” to “table”. This forces the “div” elements inside it to act more like old-school table columns, to ensure all columns have the same height. The “row div” has its “display” set to “table-cell” and surrounds the two “divs” we want to act like table cells, or columns. The “left-nav” div will display as a blue vertical bar on the left side of the screen to simulate a left-hand navigation. The “main div” is where the main content is displayed.

Now that our html template is in place, we need to tell Express which HTML engine we want to use to render html. We do this by calling the app.set() function. Enter this line of code a couple of lines underneath the line 7 call to app.use():

```
app.set('view engine', 'ejs');
```

We no longer want to use the send() function to send a response to the client browser. We want to call the ‘render()’ method, and pass it the name of the html template (minus the .ejs extension). In your code for ‘server.js’, find the get() function and delete the line containing res.send(). Replace it with the code below to call the render() function.

```
res.render('home');
```

The EJS engine is smart enough to know to look in the ‘views’ folder for a file named ‘home.ejs’. Let’s see how it looks so far. Start and re-start the node.js server and go to localhost:8080. If you see a big bold ‘NHL Teams’ in your browser, with blue nav bars, congratulations! Now let’s finish the home page code.

But before we can add html to our 'home.ejs' template file to display the team names, we must first pass the html template the data that we fetched from the NHL REST API. You do that in a second parameter to the render() function. There are two ways to do that. The first is to define as many fields as you need in an inline data object:

```
res.render('home', {fname:'Bob', lname:'Jones',
                                        middle:'A.'});
```

This strategy works fine if you have only one or two fields to pass. But I'm sure you can already tell this can quickly get cumbersome, and too long for one line of code. The second way is to define a data object and pass the whole object:

```
const person = {
  fname:'Bob',
  lname:'Jones',
  middle:'A.'
}
res.render('home', {data: person});
```

The above code defines an object called 'person' and we pass it to the render() function assigned to a 'parent' field called 'data'.

In our hockey app, we only have one data object to pass to the EJS template -- the string array of team names.

So, on line 15, update the 'res.render()' function inside the 'app.get()' function, and add the data object as the second parameter, so it looks like the following code:

```
app.get('/', async function (req, res) {
      const teamNames = await getTeams();
      res.render('home', {teamNames: teamNames});
});
```

Notice the data object we passed as the second parameter to 'res.render()'. The first 'teamNames' is the property name we will use in the EJS template to access the data. The second 'teamNames' is the name of the variable we defined in the previous line of code. Some developers like to keep the property names the same as the variable names. Others like to make them different for clarity.

The final code listing for 'server.js' should look like this:

```
import express from 'express';
import { getTeams } from './nhl.js';

const app = express();
const port = 8080;

app.use(express.json());

app.set('view engine', 'ejs');

app.listen(port, () => {
  console.log(`Hockey app listening at
                        http://localhost:${port}`);
});
```

```
app.get('/', async function (req, res) {
  const teamNames = await getTeams();
  res.render('home', {teamNames: teamNames});
});
```

Now we can go back and finish up our html template ‘home.ejs’. Open ‘home.ejs’ in VS Code. Add the following three lines of code below (in bold font) inside the “main” div, underneath the existing <h1> tag. Your code should now look like this:

```
  <div id="main">
    <h1>NHL Teams</h1>
    <% teamNames.forEach((team) => { %>
      <p><%= team %></p>
    <% }); %>
  </div>
```

Notice we added some JavaScript code embedded in the EJS html template. When you embed JavaScript, it must be between <% and %> tags. These tags are strictly for control-flow and do not render output. The first line of the JavaScript code we added just iterates the ‘teamNames’ array we passed in, with a forEach() loop, and assigns each team name to the ‘team’ parameter.

To render output with JavaScript in an EJS template, we would use the <%= and %> tags. Notice the addition of the equal sign. It is used to render output. The second line of our

JavaScript code uses these 'render' tags to output the value of the 'team' variable inside the <p> tags.

Start and restart your node server, and hopefully, after you refresh your browser, it looks like the following screenshot:

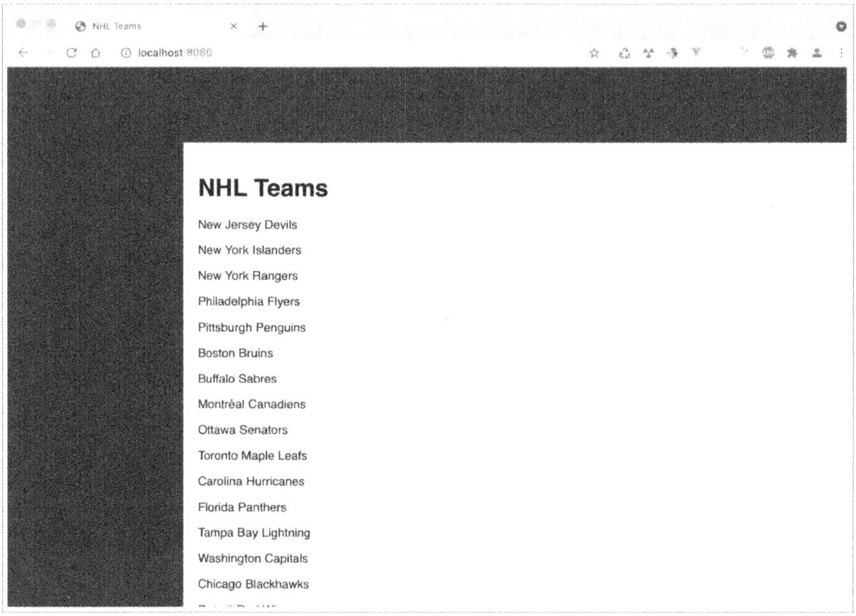

There are other tags you can use in your EJS template described in the official EJS documentation at https://ejs.co/#docs. You can even add <script> tags to your EJS template and run JavaScript code just like a normal html file.

Congratulations! You are done with the application code portion of this book. Next, we discuss how to upload and share your awesome code.

CHAPTER 8 - GITHUB

Now that you have a working Node.js project, you need to upload it to GutHub. Then you can add the GitHub url to your resume so prospective employers can view your code portfolio. Every application you write in the future can be uploaded to your code portfolio in its own project folder to keep things nice and organized.

Please note there is a difference between **Git** and **GitHub**. GitHub is a website that stores source code files in the 'cloud' (external server), known as a repository (or 'repo' for short). Git is the command-line source-control software that tracks changes to your source code files and uploads (pushes) code files from your computer to the GitHub web site. In this way, git acts as an interface between your local computer and the GitHub web site.

Command-line software means it runs in a terminal window and you type in text commands to use its features. There are software apps, like 'Sourcetree', that provide a screen of buttons and menus that issue the git commands for you behind-the-scenes. Even Visual Studio Code has built-in support for git, but its kinda janky to set up. But besides that, its important to learn the git commands because prospective employers will be much more impressed if you know the actual git commands to upload (push) source files to GitHub. So to that end, we are going to learn the basic git commands.

Each time you edit and push (upload) a source file to GitHub, it saves the new version as well as the old version, so you have a history of all the changes made to that source file. This file history is very useful when trying to track down recent code changes that may be responsible for bugs.

GitHub is arguably the most popular code **repository.** Many use GitHub to store their code, including big corporations with large development teams. These code stores are called repositories, or 'repos' for short.

The other popular code repo is bitbucket.org. It also supports git, as well as Mercurial, another source control software that is an alternative to using git. Bitbucket is developed by a company called Atlassian and is tightly integrated with bitbucket's project management software called **Jira**. We will be using git in this book, though that is not a reflection on bitbucket.

CREATE GITHUB ACCOUNT

The first thing you need to do is create a GitHub account. As with any website, it may change over time. Buttons, links and menus move or disappear. So its important to keep in mind that sometimes you may have to find things yourself.

Go to GitHub.com and click the 'sign up' button. Then you will need to enter your email address, select a password, and enter a username. You might be asked to solve a silly puzzle to prove you're not a software bot. GitHub sends a code to your email address, which you have to type-in to proceed. Then you are asked about team members, but just scroll to the bottom and click the "skip personalization" link.

You should then see the GitHub project screen (as shown in the following screenshot).

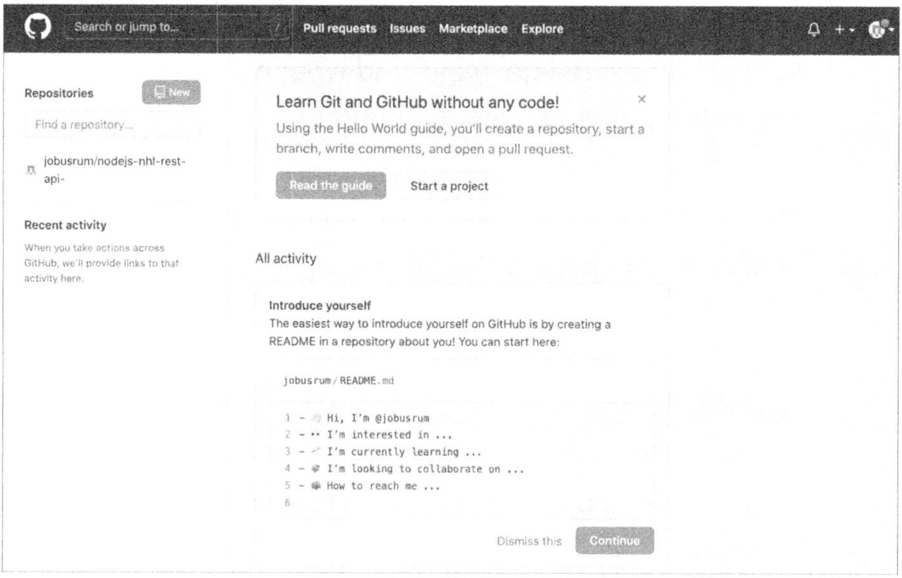

GITHUB MASTER BRANCH

Before we get started, let's change the default branch name. For PC reasons, GitHub changed the name of the default branch from 'master' to 'main'. This is fine, but all the git help you will search for on the internet will use the branch name 'master' in the example commands (because that name has been around forever). It can be really confusing to a new user why a git command doesn't work, and they may not realize it's because the branch names are different (learned this the hard way). So, click the 'Profile' icon (as shown in the following screenshot).

Choose 'Settings' from the drop-down menu. Then click 'Repositories' in the left-hand navigation panel.

In the text box, delete 'main' and type: master.
Then click the gray "Update" button.

Then click the profile icon again and choose 'Your repositories' from the drop-down menu.

GITHUB REPO

We need to create an empty repo to store the source code for your node application. Click the green "New" button.

You will need to enter a project name. This project name will become part of the GitHub url to your code repo that you will paste in your resume. So, the repo name should be descriptive of the technology used as well as the app. Since the project name becomes part of the url to your portfolio, it must also be unique in your account. Enter a repo name of 'nodejs-nhl-rest-api'.

We want prospective employers to be able to access this code repo, so we will click the “Public” radio button.

Check the box for “Add a README file”. It will add a blank readme file to the root of your repo. A readme file lets you enter a project summary for visitors to your code repo. For example, you might describe the technologies used, explain what each file does, maybe add some screenshots. GitHub readme’s are written in a markup language roughly similar to HTML. We will create our own readme in the next chapter.

Uncheck the box for “Add a .gitignore” file since we will add one later to our Visual Studio Code project.

Click the green “Create repository” button.

GIT SSH CONFIG

Your laptop will use the SSH protocol to connect to GitHub instead of the less secure HTTPS protocol. So we need to open up a terminal and configure your git credentials, then create an SSH key that we will copy and paste to our GitHub account. This is not hard to do, but it does involve many steps. So open a terminal window and ‘cd’ into your project’s root folder.

Set your git username (to whatever username you used to create your GitHub account)

```
> git config --global user.name "bob"
```

Then set your git email (to whatever email address you used to create your GitHub account)

```
> git config --global user.email bob@domain.com
```

Now we must create your public/private RSA key pair files. Running the command below creates a 'public key' file and a 'private key' file. You keep the private file a secret on your hard drive, and give the public key file to entities that require it (like GitHub). Both files will be saved in the '.ssh' folder. When you are asked to name the files, just press Enter key to accept the default name of 'id_rsa'. (If you previously set up a key with that name, you can use a different name.) You will also be asked to enter a 'passphrase' (twice). This is like a password, so you will need to remember it, because git asks you to enter it many times. When you are ready to create your public/private RSA key pair files, run the following command:

```
> ssh-keygen
```

Next you need to clear the stored ssh cache before adding. This is optional because it removes any old, orphaned identities, but is a good idea to prevent issues.

```
> ssh-add -D
```

Now, add your SSH key to the ssh-agent, using the name you used to create the file. (You will be asked for your passphrase).

ssh-add ~/.ssh/id_rsa

Now we're going to copy the RSA *public* key to the clipboard (so we can paste it into our GitHub account). Notice that a '.pub' extension is added to the 'public key' file name. Therefore, 'id_rsa' would be your private key. And 'id_rsa.pub' would be your public key.

> cat ~/.ssh/id_rsa.pub | pbcopy

GITHUB SSH

Now we need to paste the SSH public key into your GitHub account. Go back to the GitHub web site in your browser, and click the 'Profile' icon (as shown in the following screenshot).

Choose 'Settings' from the drop-down menu. Then click 'SSH & GPG keys' in the left-hand navigation panel. Then click the green "New SSH key" button.

Give it a descriptive name that lets you know what device uses this key. Enter 'mac laptop key'. Then paste your public key contents (that you copied from the terminal) into the 'Key' text box. Then click the green “Add SSH key” button. (You might have to enter your GitHub password again).

To test if you’ve got everything set up correctly on your laptop, enter this command in the terminal:

```
> ssh -T git@github.com
```

If you see this message “Hi [username]! You've successfully authenticated, but GitHub does not provide shell access.” That is good. If the message contains your username, everything is set up correctly. You just don’t want to see any message that says ‘permission denied’.

GIT INITIALIZE

We need to let git know it needs to monitor our project folder for any code changes to our source files. We do this with the ‘git init’ command. So open up a terminal window, and ‘cd’ into the root level of your project directory.

```
> git init
```

This will add a folder named ‘.git’ to your project folder. This is how git tracks modifications to your code. It should remain invisible to the Finder since the filename starts with a dot (unless you have the Finder configured to display hidden files).

GIT IGNORE

A git ignore file is where we list all the files and folders we don't want to push to our code repo. Things like the node_modules folder, system files and build files in the project folder. We need to add a git ignore file to our project.

Switch back to Visual Studio Code. Click the 'Source Control' icon in the skinny left-hand navigation panel, as shown by the red arrow in the screenshot below.

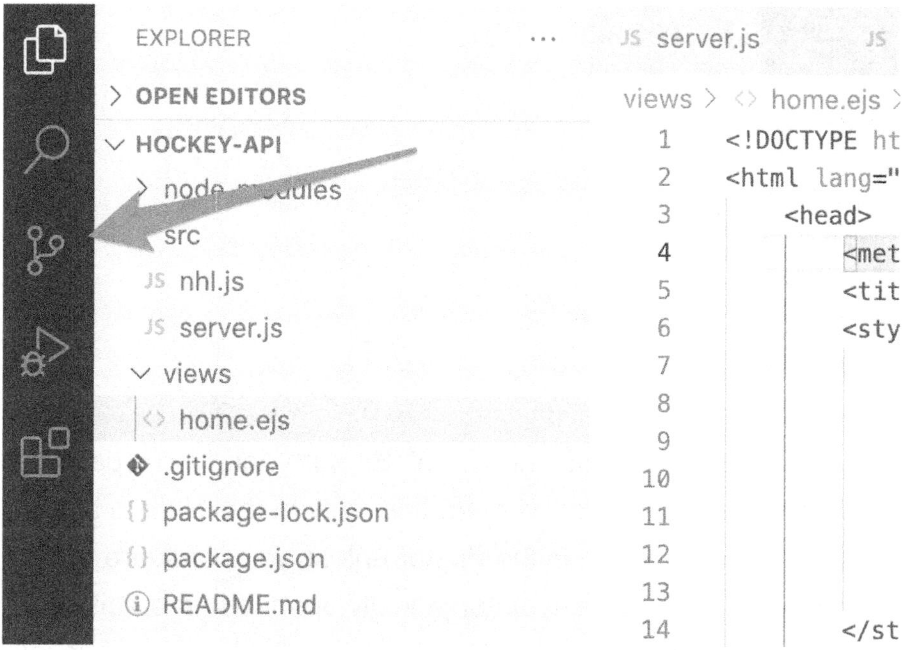

Notice that the Source Control Explorer suddenly displays 500+ files that it is ready to push to the GitHub web site, even though we only created six source files! That's because git thinks we want to upload the node_modules folder. Recall that the node_modules folders contains many files from third party software. We don't need to upload this large folder because it is easy to re-create from the package.json file. So let's tell GitHub we want to *exclude* the node_modules folder from our repo. We do that by adding a file named '.gitignore' to the root level of our project, and list all the files we want to exclude from our repo.

Click the 'New File' icon next to the project name.

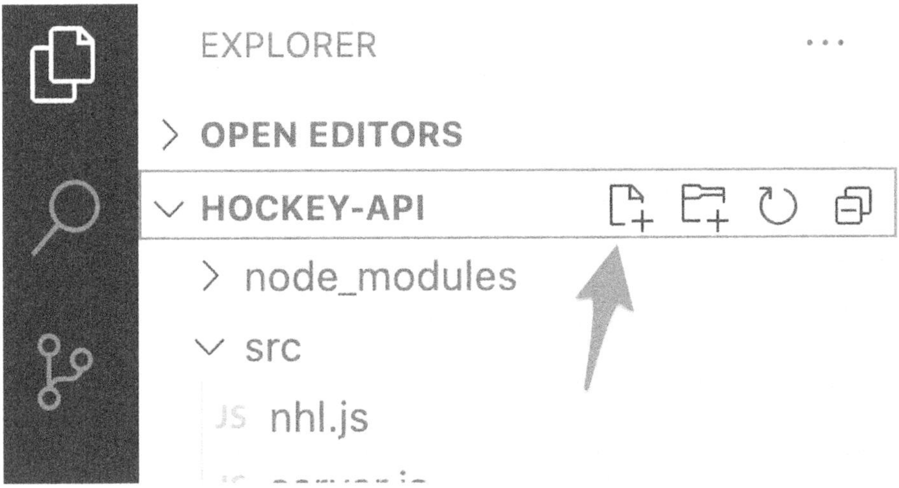

And name the file '.gitignore'. Be sure and type a period at the beginning. This tells the operating system this file is a hidden file (that won't show up in the Finder unless you configure them to display). The new file is automatically opened in the editor. Enter the basic excludes (for MacOs) listed on the next page into the '.gitignore' file and save it. (For Windows, just search Google for 'basic windows gitignore'.)

```
#####
# OS X temporary files
.DS_Store
.Trashes
*.swp

#####
# Node stuff
logs
*.log
npm-debug.log*

# Compiled binary addons
build/Release

# Dependency directory
node_modules

# Runtime data
pids
*.pid
*.seed
```

Notice we specified the 'node_modules' folder as something we want to exclude, as well as some miscellaneous files that you may or may not have in your project folder. It's a good idea to leave these other entries in the file, because you probably won't notice if/when system files and/or build files appear in the project folder.

Once you save the '.gitignore' file, Visual Studio Code automatically removes node_modules folder from the Source Control Explorer, and you are back to six files.

GIT COMMIT AND PUSH

Uploading files to GitHub is a two-stage process for git called **Commit** and **Push**. The 'commit' command tells git that a file is earmarked to be uploaded to GitHub. The 'push' command uploads a file to GitHub.

But before we can push (upload) files to GitHub, we need to the specific SSH url to the repo. To get this url, go back to GitHub in your browser, and click the 'Profile' icon (as shown in the following screenshot).

Choose 'Settings' from the drop-down menu. Then click 'Your repositories' in the left-hand navigation panel. And then click the repo name 'nodejs-nhl-rest-api'. Click the green "Code" button and it should display a drop-down window, as shown in the following screenshot.

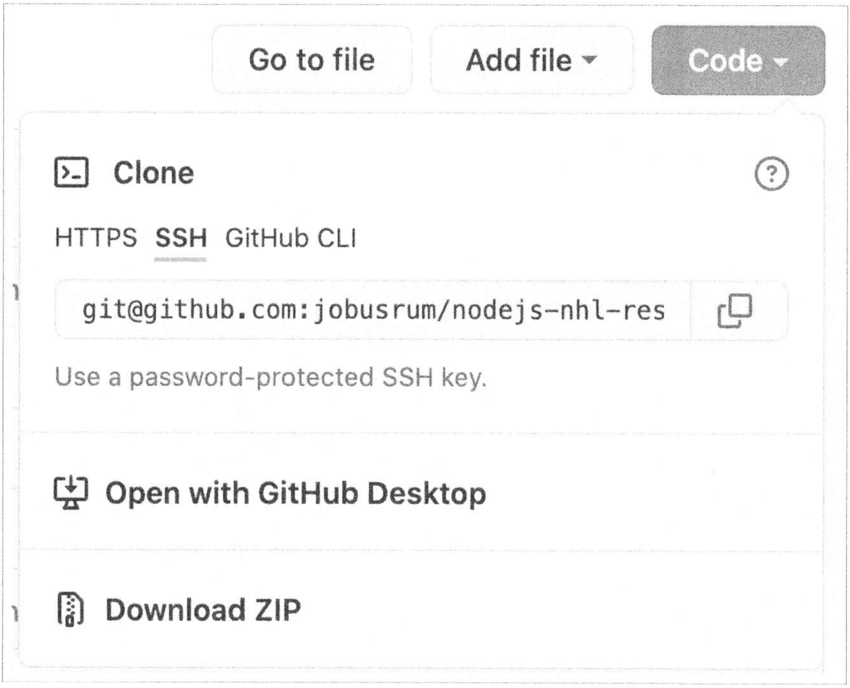

If the 'SSH' tab is not already underlined, click on it. Then click on the double-square icon on the right and it will copy the url to your clipboard.

Switch to your terminal and enter the command, replacing '[ssh url]' with the SSH url you just copied.

> git remote add origin [ssh url]

First thing you should do is a ‘pull’ request by entering the command below. This will download any new files in the repo that are not yet in your local git repo, such as the readme we added from the GitHub website. (You may have to enter your passphrase).

```
> git pull origin master
```

You have to tell git which files that you want to push to GitHub by adding them to a ‘commit’. Notice the dot at the end of the command below. The dot means add *all* the files that have been modified since the last push. Otherwise you would specify individual files by name.

```
> git add .
```

Next, you have to execute the ‘commit’ command.
The ‘-m’ flag adds a commit message.

```
> git commit -m "initial upload"
```

The terminal will display a list of all files that were added to the commit. Now you need to ‘push’ them to GitHub. (You may have to enter your passphrase).

```
> git push
```

If you get an error that says "The current branch master has no upstream branch", enter the command below. (You may have to enter your passphrase).

> git push --set-upstream origin master

Then try another 'push' by pressing the up arrow key until the previous 'push' command is displayed and press the Enter key.

Go back to your GitHub repo page in your browser, and refresh the page. You should now see that all the files have been uploaded to your repo.

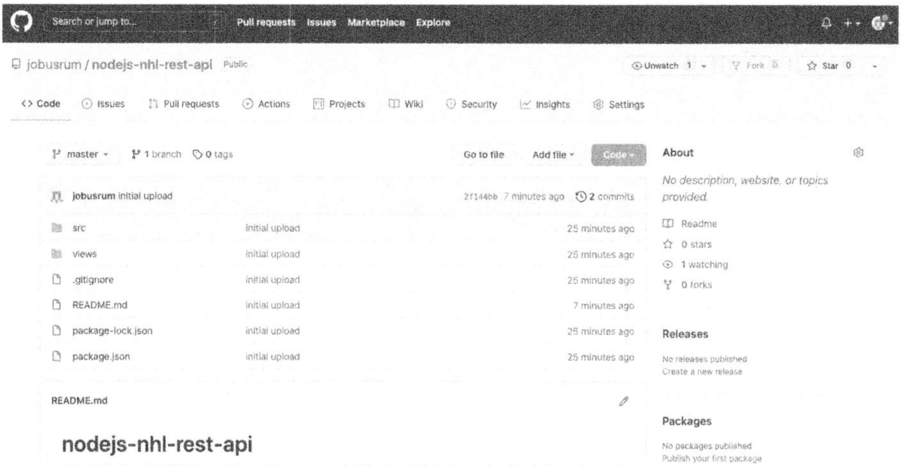

There is one file that we do not want in our repo that we need to delete. Let's do this in the GutHub web site. Click on the 'src' folder. Click on the 'test.js' file. Then click the trash can icon to delete the file (as shown in the next screenshot).

Type a name for this commit, such as: delete test file

And click the green ‘Commit Changes’ button.

The file is gone from your GitHub repo, but not from your local repo. So switch back to the terminal and pull the latest commits, which includes the commit that deletes the test file. (You may have to enter your passphrase).

> git pull

Now, switch back to Visual Studio Code’s File Explorer. Click the Source Control Explorer icon, as shown in the next screenshot.

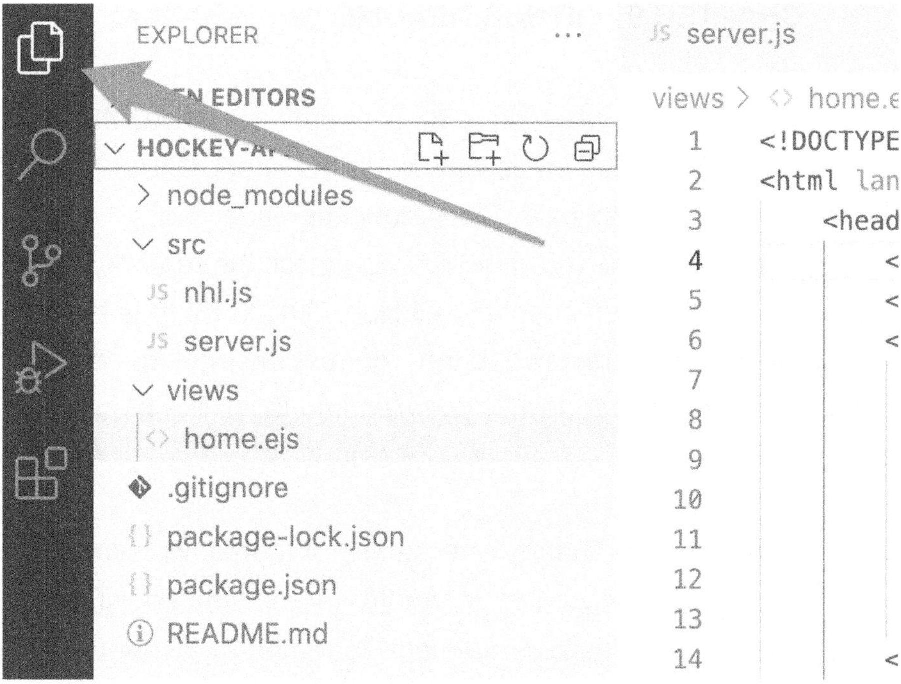

You will see that the 'test.js' file is now gone from your local repo. And you should also notice that the 'README.md' file has also been added to your project (from the pull request you ran).

CHAPTER 9 - GITHUB README

The last thing we need to do is update the **README** file. This is time-consuming but is well worth the effort. GitHub readme's use a syntax called Markdown to render the 'readme.md' file in the browser. You *could* edit the readme in Visual Studio and then push it to GitHub. But GitHub has a cool online editor with a preview tab that renders the markup code in real-time so you can see what your readme looks like before you commit the changes.

Here are some handy references for Markdown syntax:

- https://docs.github.com/en/rest/reference/markdown
- https://docs.github.com/en/github/writing-on-github/getting-started-with-writing-and-formatting-on-github/basic-writing-and-formatting-syntax

Don't be frustrated if writing the readme takes almost as long as the code itself. Make sure you proofread the text and edit any awkward statements, and fix typos. This is your code portfolio and in many ways, is the first impression you will make with a prospective employer. Your 'readme' is essentially YOU explaining to the BOSS how you wrote the code, what your code does, and what technologies you used. So put in the time and effort to create a kick-ass 'readme'.

With that said, it's time to edit that readme. Go back to the GitHub repo page in your browser, the one that displays all the files. If you scroll down, you'll see the 'readme' page displayed.

There isn't much there yet, just the project title. To edit this page, click on the 'pencil' in the upper-right corner of the 'readme' display.

In the online markup code editor, you'll see one line of code. As shown below, this line of code displays the project name in a large font, or 'Heading 1':

```
# nodejs-nhl-rest-api
```

In Markdown, one hashtag displays a 'Heading 1'. Two hashtags display a 'Heading 2', and so on, right down to six hashtags to display a 'Heading 6'. Make sure there is a space between the hashtag and the text, or it won't render properly. Change the title to:

```
# NHL REST API in Node.js
```

Press Enter a couple times to create new lines. Then click the "Preview" tab to see how the change looks. When you are done, click the "Edit file" tab to go back into edit mode.

Next, we want to add an overview/description of the project, which can just be typed as regular text, no markdown required. Try to write your overviews as if an employer asked you "so what does this project do?" You might write something like this, on line 3:

```
	This hockey application is written in Node.js. It
uses the Axios package to call the REST API of nhl.com,
```

```
and parses the JSON results to extract team names. It
uses the "Embedded JavaScript" (EJS) engine to generate
HTML. It then uses Express to handle web requests and
send the web page to the browser.
```

View how these changes look in the preview tab. Then go back to edit mode.

Notice all the buzz words we injected in the description: Node.js, Express, Axios, REST API, JSON. Be sure and pepper your resume and/or online portfolio (like GitHub or Linked-in) with buzz words of every technology you've used. Large online job recruiters, such as cybercoders.com, use AI to scan resumes for buzz words and how frequently they are found in your resume. This helps them match up an applicant's skill level with their job listings. For example, a resume that mentions JavaScript once, may only be a 10% match for a Node.js position. But another resume that lists JavaScript and Node.js in three projects, as well as Express and Axios may be an 80% match for the same job.

Let's add some hyperlinks for each source file, and explain their purpose. To create links, use this syntax:

```
[Link Text](url/to/file.js)
```

The text of the link goes inside square brackets. The url goes inside parenthesis. Enter the markdown below to add a link for each file, along with a quick description of what it does, and put it inside an un-numbered list (which is done with a hyphen and a space).

```
    - [nhl.js](src/nhl.js) - This file is responsible
for using Axios to call the nhl.com REST API. It then
parses the JSON to extract team names, and returns a JSON
array to the caller.

    - [views/home.ejs](views/home.ejs) - This file is
the EJS template that accepts a string array, and then
iterates through it to display the team name.

    - [server.js](src/server.js) - This file is
responsible for configuring a server to respond to web
requests on port 8080. It contains a 'get' handler that
calls a method in 'nhl.js', which returns data from a
REST API/ It then sends that data to the EJS html engine,
which returns the generated HTML to the browser.
```

Go to preview mode to make sure it renders and looks correct, then go back into edit mode. Now let's add a screenshot image to spice things up. Images are added by typing an exclamation point ! and wrapping the alt text inside square brackets [ ]. The image url is then placed inside parentheses (). No space between the brackets and the parenthesis, or the image will not render. The syntax looks like this:

```
![This is an image](https://exp.com/img/mypic.svg)
```

But before we add the markdown for the image, we must first create an ‘images’ folder in our GitHub repo, and then upload an image to the folder. We can easily do this in the GitHub web site.

Creating a folder on the GitHub web site must happen together with adding at least a single file (which you can delete later). This is because git doesn't track empty folders. You must define a new folder by typing in the desired path of the new file. For example, if we add a new ‘readme’ file with a path of "/images/readme.md" and then 'commit' it, it will create both a new folder named ‘images’, and a new ‘readme.md’ file. Later, you can either delete the ‘readme’ file (with a new commit) or leave it blank.

Go to the repo's main page, that lists all the source files, and click the "Add file" button. Then click “Create new file”. In the text box that says ‘Name your file’, type in the filename with path:

/images/readme.md

Notice how the leading slash automatically added a folder to the path name. Scroll down to the commit section, and add a commit message, such as "added images directory". Then click the green "Commit new file" button.

You should be redirected to a page showing the contents of the 'images' folder. Now we can upload an image from our hard drive by clicking the “Add File” button, and then click “Upload files”. This takes you to the upload page.

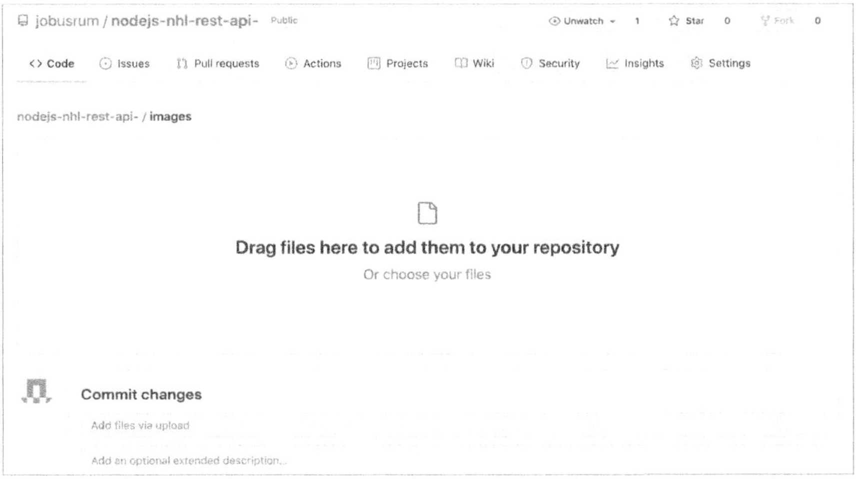

I assume you already took a screenshot of your browser page. If not, you can just search for “macos how to take screenshot”.

You can either drag a file from your hard drive onto the browser screen, or click the blue “choose your files” link to open a file browser dialog. After choosing your screenshot image file, you must commit this change, just like you would when using git in the terminal. Write a commit message in the textbox, such as:

```
uploaded screenshot for readme.
```

Click the radio button for “Commit directly to the master branch”, then click the green “Commit changes” button.

Now your screenshot is in your images folder, so its now ready to display on your main 'readme'. Go back to your repo's main page, and scroll down to click the pencil icon to edit the 'readme'.

Underneath the hyperlinks, type the markdown below to display the screenshot from the images folder. (Make sure you use whatever filename you gave to your screenshot image file. I named my 'NHL_Teams.png'.

```
![Screenshot](/images/NHL_Teams.png)
```

Scroll down, add a commit message like "added screenshot" and click the green "Commit changes" button.

Now try clicking the links in your 'readme' and make sure they take you to the appropriate view source page.

Pro tip: if you ever visit someone else's repo source files, and you want to copy and paste some of their code, click the gray "Raw" button. It displays the raw code, suitable for selecting and copying.

Now you need to download the files you created on the GitHub web site to your local repo. You can do this with git, so open up a terminal, and issue the 'pull' command.

> git pull

If you go back to VS Code, you should now see some new files in your file explorer. The new 'readme' you created should be in the root of your project folder. Also notice there is now an images folder with your screenshot inside.

You should make of habit of always doing a 'git pull' every time you work on code to get the latest updated code files in your local repo.

Your GitHub profile repo is now complete. To get a url to copy into your resume, or email a prospective employer, go to the main repo page, and copy the url from your browser's text box. It will looking something like this:

https://github.com/jobusrum/nodejs-nhl-rest-api

Notice after the GitHub domain name, comes your username, followed by the repo name. All GitHub repo urls use this format.

CHAPTER 10 - NVM

Before I let you go, I want to introduce you to the **Node Version Manager** (**NVM**). If you're curious, their GitHub repo is:

https://github.com/nvm-sh/nvm

The node version manager allows you to run several different versions of node on your computer. Since node.js is a framework, lots of applications are built 'on top' of node.js. That means they require node.js installed on your computer before they can run. Sometimes, these apps are locked into a specific version of node.js. So you may end up downloading a node.js application but when you go to run it, it displays an error saying 'your version of node.js is not supported', or 'you're using the wrong version of node'.

That's where NVM comes in. NVM makes it super easy to install a new version of node.js right from your terminal. Or switch to a different version of node.

It's best to install NVM by downloading the install script. For older Macs, a 'bash' script was run from the terminal. However newer Macs use zsh instead of bash. So if you're using an older mac with bash, you have to install NVM a little differently by first creating a bash_profile, then running a command to download and run the script. Finally, a third command refreshes the available commands in your system path. The three commands to run are:

> touch ~/.bash_profile

(This second command should be typed all on one line, even it it wraps to the next line. FYI: that is a 'pipe' character before the word 'bash', and not a capital 'I'. Also, don't forget the period, when typing 'install.sh'.)

> curl -o- https://raw.githubusercontent.com/creationix/nvm/v0.39.0/install.sh | bash

> source ~/.nvm/nvm.sh

To check that NVM was installed successfully, run this command:

> nvm --version

NVM can easily install a different version of node.js. Just issue the command and name the version you want.

> nvm install 14.15.4

NVM also makes it very easy to switch to another version of node.js. Just run this command with the version number you want to switch to:

> nvm use 12

To see what versions of node.js are currently installed on your machine:

```
> nvm ls
```

To see what versions of node.js are available to download, run this command:

```
> nvm ls-remote
```

Now you are up-to-speed with the Node Version Manager.

Conclusion

And so we come to the end of this book. You have learned how node.js functions and are now competent enough to 'jump right in' and contribute to a node.js project at work. Or develop your own node.js application. No doubt you will have to continue your own research as you come across functions and libraries in a code base that you are not yet familiar with. But that is true no matter what framework or programming language you are using.

Sockets.io

In other ways, we have barely scratched the surface of node.js and the libraries and packages that make it so powerful. One such library is 'sockets.io', which allow *two-way* communication between the server and the client. Traditionally, a client, such as a browser, connects to a server and requests data. The server sends the content to the client. That's one-way communication, or half-duplex. With sockets.io, once connected to a server, a client can send messages and events back to the server. That's two-way communication, or full-duplex.

Most tutorials for socket.io start with a multi-user chat application but the uses for socket.io are endless – games, peer-to-peer applications, or the next great social media destination! You're only limited by your imagination. You would benefit greatly from putting one of those socket.io tutorials on your to-do list.

Static Files

Another thing we did not discuss much was **static files**. Static files are those web files that serve up the same content every time, such as image files, video files, html files, css files, csv files, JSON data files. This is opposed to dynamic files that may serve up customized content by going to the database and fetching saved data for the current user.

In node.js, static files are kept in a single subdirectory, most commonly named 'public'. Your code accesses these files with help of the 'path' package. Use the import statement:

```
import path from 'path';
```

Then you can set a variable that points to the full path name of the 'public' directory.

```
const staticFiles = path.join(__dirname, 'public');
```

The global variable '**__dirname**' stores the directory path containing the currently executing file (global variables begin with *two* underscores). Then 'path.join' is used to combine everything in the parenthesis into one path. Now your code may use the 'staticFiles' variable whenever it needs to load a static file.

C-Ya

And so we come to the end. Just remember your ABC's: Always be coding!!!

Made in the USA
Monee, IL
04 November 2026

67378044R00059